Washed Up!

Written by Payal Kapadia
Illustrated by Robin Boyden

Published by Pearson Education Limited, 80 Strand, London, WC2R 0RL.

www.pearsonschools.co.uk

Text © Pearson Education Limited 2016

Original illustrations © Pearson Education Limited

Illustrated by Robin Boyden

First published in the USA by Pearson Education Inc, 2016

First published in the UK by Pearson Education Ltd, 2017

25

10 9

British Library Cataloguing in Publication Data

A catalogue record for this book is available from the British Library

ISBN 9780435164386

Copyright notice

All rights reserved. No part of this publication may be reproduced in any form or by any means (including photocopying or storing it in any medium by electronic means and whether or not transiently or incidentally to some other use of this publication) without the written permission of the copyright owner, except in accordance with the provisions of the Copyright, Designs and Patents Act 1988 or under the terms of a licence issued by the Copyright Licensing Agency, Barnards Inn, 86 Fetter Lane, London EC4A 1EN (www.cla.co.uk). Applications for the copyright owner's written permission should be addressed to the publisher.

Acknowledgements

We would like to thank Bangor Central Integrated Primary, NI; Parkfield Primary School, Manchester; St Matthew's CE Primary, Stretton; Bishop Henderson CE Primary, Somerset; Bridge Learning Campus, Bristol; Barton Hill Academy, Devon; Southroyd Primary, Leeds; St John's CE Primary, Maidstone; Sandling Primary, Maidstone; Lingham Primary, Wirral; Foxdell Infants, Luton; Pennoweth Primary, Redruth; Clifton-Upon-Teme Primary, Clifton-Upon-Teme; Broadgreen Primary, Liverpool for their invaluable help in the development and trialling of the Bug Club resources.

Printed in the UK by Bell and Bain Ltd, Glasgow

Contents

Chapter One	4
Chapter Two	18
Chapter Three	28
Chapter Four	42
Chapter Five	49

Chapter One

"This is the Indian Ocean's best-kept SECRET! An island so far from civilisation you won't find it on any MAP! An island untouched by humans – until NOW!"

Pop sensation Berry Blue was shouting out the last word of every sentence over the din made by the Channel 16 chopper she was travelling in. She was so excited she found it hard to stay in her seat.

"What better spot for the biggest, baddest reality show on the PLANET! Welcome to . . . *WASHED UP!*" What Berry Blue said next was drowned out by the wind.

"Did you get a picture with her?" Shen's mother asked, leaning forward in her seat. "She looks famous!"

Shen Liu bit down hard on his tongue. It wouldn't be appropriate to be cheeky to his mum, but she was clamoring for a photo without even the faintest idea who Berry Blue was . . . and *everyone* knew who Berry Blue was!

"She's a little glamorous for the middle of nowhere, isn't she?" commented Shen's twin sister Mei.

"She's not setting foot on the island, silly!" said Shen, directing his irritation at her. "She's the host of the program. Shhhh, listen!"

"Thousands of families competed for the chance to be a part of *Washed Up!* – the planet's most talked-about survivor series," Berry Blue was now saying, "and out of all our applicants, three families showed that they have what it takes. I have the first contestants, the lovely Lius, here with me now!"

"Smile!" hissed Mrs Liu as the cameras turned towards the family and she posed in a practised way.

"The other two families, the Walpoles and the Garcias, are travelling by boat to the other side of the island," continued Berry Blue. She had the attention of the cameras again before they zoomed in on the sleek speedboat slicing through the unending turquoise waters far below. "Three unknown environments await these families, and three survival kits — one with a mosquito net, others with a length of rope. Then there are tarpaulins, matches, and knives for everyone."

"For three weeks, our contestants must rely on themselves and no one else. The winners get a book deal, a round-the-world book tour, and a generous cash prize . . . but, of course, to win they'll need your votes, and they'll need to make it out ALIVE!"

"And they will, RIGHT?" She winked at the camera. "So here it is, the ISLAND! Isn't it GORGEOUS?"

The island rose up before their eyes like an emerald-green sea monster. There was a golden strip of sandy beach, a mountain wreathed in mist, and a lush jungle. Shen and Mei gasped.

"This island is the ultimate survival challenge for our contestants," said Berry Blue, batting her eyelashes as the helicopter dipped lower. "If they adapt to life here, they could win the contest. If they don't, who knows what might happen!"

"Like she knows anything about survival," muttered Shen, but Mei silenced him with a look. The cameras were on them now as they alighted on a wind-whipped mountain slope, while Berry Blue waved goodbye wildly.

"You'd better watch what you say," whispered Mei, as both children took in the flying cameras hovering over the island, "because we're on TV from now until we leave!"

"Well, I was only about to say that down there, it looks like a tropical paradise!" cried Shen. His eyes were dazzled by the sweep of ocean far below the mountain, the sun glinting off the waves.

Down below, fresh off the speedboat, Mr Walpole was about to say the same thing, but his wife beat him to it.

"Sun, sand, sea!" she exclaimed. "There's nothing like the simple pleasures in life!"

Oliver rolled his eyes. His parents holidayed at fancy hotels that had posh restaurants and spas offering beauty treatments. What did they know about *simple*?

The speedboat turned away with the Garcias still on board, bound for the coastal mangroves. The Garcias watched the Walpoles walking towards the cool shade of the rain forest, across a sliver-thin strip of blazing hot sand. Then their boat rounded a bend, and they were all alone.

It was deathly silent as the skipper cut the engine, letting the boat glide gently into the mangrove swamp that would be home to the Garcias for the next three weeks. Mr Garcia gazed at the muddy sludge around him, his jaw twitching.

"It'll be OK, Papa!" lied Gabriela, as she surveyed the murky water, so shallow that the gnarled roots of the trees writhed like snakes above the waterline.

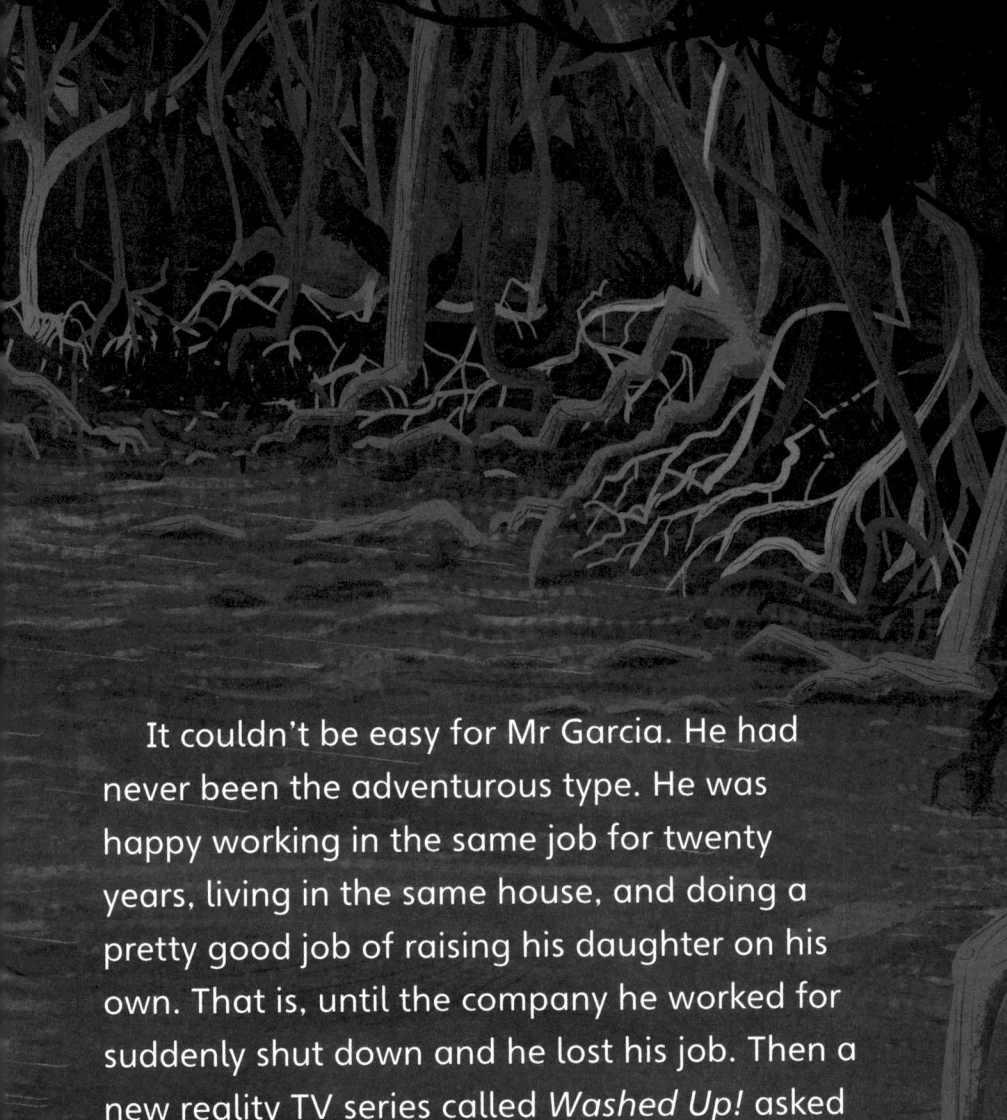

It couldn't be easy for Mr Garcia. He had never been the adventurous type. He was happy working in the same job for twenty years, living in the same house, and doing a pretty good job of raising his daughter on his own. That is, until the company he worked for suddenly shut down and he lost his job. Then a new reality TV series called *Washed Up!* asked for volunteers, and Gabriela's father did the unthinkable – he applied.

"The tide will come in soon," said Gabriela, squinting at the solid wall of roots stretching out in front of them, "so we'd better find higher ground."

Meanwhile, the Lius were doing some climbing of their own. The helicopter had dropped them off next to a steep mountain slope. Shen and Mei were as nimble as mountain goats, but Mr and Mrs Liu kept stopping to wave at the cameras, and to catch their breath.

Mei shivered. The wind was vicious above the tree line. Far above them loomed the snow-covered volcano. Right now it was hard to imagine that this was once the site of a powerful eruption spewing red-hot lava for miles around.

"There's not enough wood here to build both a fire and a shelter," said Shen. The Liu siblings had seen enough survival shows to know that they would need both soon.

Mei glanced up. The sun would go down over the mountain in a few hours. "We'll head downhill first thing tomorrow, to where the tree cover thickens," she said.

"That's fine," said Mr Liu. "Now blow a kiss to the camera!"

Closer to sea level, Oliver Walpole hurried his mother past the scorpion scuttling across the forest floor. His mother's island euphoria would give way to utter panic if she saw any of these nasties.

"It's marvellous, isn't it!" she exclaimed, oblivious of the scorpions. *Suffocating* would have been a better word to describe it, Oliver thought. It was hotter here than on the beach, even though only a chink of greenish light pierced the forest canopy.

"Here, let me wash that!" Mrs Walpole screeched, and before Oliver could stop her, Mrs Walpole had spilled half their thermos of water on the small fruit he had just picked up.

"You shouldn't have done that, Mum!" he protested, loudly. His heart sank – their water rations were down to half already.

Many miles away, Berry Blue, in an animal print dress now, was speaking to the cameras again. "Don't they look like they're having so much fun?" she purred. "Things always start out that way . . ."

Her eyes glinted sharply as she said, ". . . but their rations will soon run out, and daylight too, and then darkness, hunger, and thirst will set in."

Here she tittered, "And that's when the real fun begins, dear viewers! It only gets better – or *worse!*"

CHAPTER TWO

"As I predicted, in so little time, so much has changed!" Perhaps Berry Blue was referring to her hairdo, woven with leaves to make her look like a forest nymph.

Now the Walpoles were on the TV screen, and they didn't cut as pretty a picture. Mrs Walpole had just emitted a blood-curdling cry that shook the forest to its roots after a spider had used her hand as a landing pad.

"We need a fire to keep creepy-crawlies away," said Mr Walpole frantically.

Oliver inhaled deeply. "Dad, the matches are all wet."

"Oh, great, let's play the blame game!" said Harvey Walpole. "Your mother was half-drowning in the waves, and you wanted me to think about the matches!"

The water they'd waded through to come ashore had only been knee-deep, but Oliver bit his lip. This was probably not the best time to make a point.

"It's too sticky for a fire anyway," said Mrs Walpole, lifting one perfectly arched eyebrow, "and it makes my hair frizz!"

Oliver said nothing. He was looking at the jungle canopy towering above them like a thirty-storey building. *Up* – it seemed the only way to escape a forest floor teeming with bugs was to go up, but the thought of it made him a little light-headed. He stared at the buttress roots propping up the tallest trees, and masses of vines and creepers that looked like spaghetti.

The thought of food made Oliver's stomach rumble. The creepers weren't for eating, but they were as thick as a man's arm, twisting and twining up to the sun. Maybe they had other uses . . .

"Let's make a camp," he shouted. "We can cut these creepers and build somewhere to sleep!"

"I'll handle that!" said Mr Walpole gallantly, and Oliver heaved an inward sigh of relief. The family row had been postponed, at least for now.

Mr Garcia was also looking up, which explained why his foot got caught in a mess of tangled roots. His ankle throbbed painfully, but his heart jumped. Water, food, fuel, and shelter. This was it!

"Coconut palms!" said Gabriela, feeling thankful for the coconuts that had travelled across oceans and on currents to take root on this remote island. She shot her father a worried look as he extricated his foot, wincing. "Are you OK, Papa?"

He nodded, although a red-hot flash of pain surged through his leg as they trudged forward, the mud sucking around their feet. The tide was coming in faster than they'd expected, submerging their swampy jetty and threatening to overcome them. Sprained ankle or not, they would have to keep moving, even if every movement was excruciatingly slow.

They clambered to dry land as the tide rose higher. "We'll tie palm leaves together for our shelter here," said Gabriela, recalling all the survival adventures she'd watched on TV and read about in books. They made it look so easy!

"We can save some palm fronds to go underneath us and keep us warm," she said and saw the agreement on her father's face. Then he looked away. Gabriela's father had never stepped out of the little town where he was born, and now they were in a mangrove swamp. There would be rising tides and hungry crocodiles, as well as the leeches and snakes that she hoped the palm fronds would protect them from. Gabriela was glad she didn't have to spell it out for him.

was only enough bread, cheese, and raisins to last one whole day, *if* they ate frugally. The temperature had dropped noticeably, and the wind whistled like a banshee.

Mrs Liu's teeth were chattering already. "Look w-w-warm!" she stuttered, still sparing a frozen smile for the flying cameras. Mr Liu's speech was slurred. "No a-animal c-can s-ssurvive th-thissss."

The twins exchanged looks – early signs of *hypothermia*. They had to find shelter, and fast.

Shen's thoughts were wandering again: How did animals survive in this windy wasteland of grass and rock?

"Gelada baboons!" said Mei, reading Shen's thoughts as always. Didn't these mountain-dwelling primates escape their windswept habitat by climbing down steep cliff faces at nightfall and roosting in ledges?

The minutes were slipping away as fast as their body heat now, and Shen knew the cold, thin air was making it hard for him to think.

"Follow ussss!" Shen cried out to his parents. Mei was pulling the tarpaulins out of their bags, her hands fumbling with the zip.

Shen had a plan now, but he needed a tree for this to work, and there were no trees so far above the tree line. Could he use a rock, maybe? Or three, an outcrop of three rocks, now *that* would work. Dizzy now, Shen felt the wind stinging his eyes as he peered over the edge of the mountain to look at a narrow sill, only a few feet down. It would do . . . it would have to.

"Now isn't that *ingenious!*" Berry Blue, in army fatigues now, was clapping. The Lius were tucked inside two large tarpaulin hammocks slung over the cliff, moored by rocks. Below them, a tiny ledge stood between them and nothingness.

"There's always a solution to every problem," Berry Blue said, tilting her head thoughtfully to one side. The Garcias were crawling into their palm-leaf shelter, and the Walpoles were already inside a large structure made of creepers suspended above the ground.

"So safe, so sound," said Berry Blue, pretending to yawn and hugging her heart-shaped pillow. "Good night, and oh, sleep tight!"

CHAPTER THREE

In her white silk jumpsuit with a paw print across the front, Berry Blue looked radiant and rested.

"It's a lovely morning on *Washed Up!*" she said, and then her face dropped theatrically. "But not for everyone. Welcome to day fifteen!"

The morning was like a sauna for the Walpoles; hot, damp, and suffocating. It was their second week on the island, but there was no getting used to the cramped sleeping quarters, or the darkness. They hadn't seen the sky in days.

"I have to brush my teeth!" complained Mrs Walpole. She had felt nauseous all night after drinking scummy water from a standing pool.

Their water rations were almost down to nothing, but nevertheless Oliver handed his mother the thermos. "Happy Birthday, Mum," he said feebly. It was easy to lose track of time here . . . was he the only one who remembered that his mum's fortieth birthday was what had brought them here in the first place? "A paradise island, darling! Sun, sand, sea . . . doesn't it sound perfect?" he remembered her saying to his father while she read the application form.

"I would raise a toast to you turning forty, my dear, but you've finished all the water!" said Mr Walpole sourly.

Mrs Walpole glared at him. "Excuse me for supposing this would be a change from the dull birthday parties you throw me every year! Thanks to you, we'll go hungry!"

Oliver cringed. The family row had resumed. Worms, bats, and monkeys had claimed all the ripe fruit that fell to the forest floor. Oliver had built a steady pile of raw fruit, but Mr Walpole had left it unguarded while they searched for water, and now most of it was gone.

It was the dry season, and they'd found a tiny stream at long last, but Mrs Walpole insisted they keep moving. Since they'd arrived they'd shifted camp four times, but no one knew where they were supposed to be going. Without clear sight of the sun, they were lost.

They were walking in glum silence, slipping in the underbrush, getting scraped by thorns, when out of nowhere a sea breeze broke the stillness.

"The beach!" Oliver cried. They'd been walking in circles, and now they were back where they'd started.

They stared at the blue glimmer of the sea, but Oliver's parents had no strength to keep going. They decided to stop and rest.

"I'll walk down to the beach and see what I can find," said Oliver, eager to get away.

"Get us some new matches!" shouted Mrs Walpole behind him, as though he were off to the supermarket.

"Because I'm to blame for getting the old ones wet!" Mr Walpole was muttering, but he was out of Oliver's earshot now.

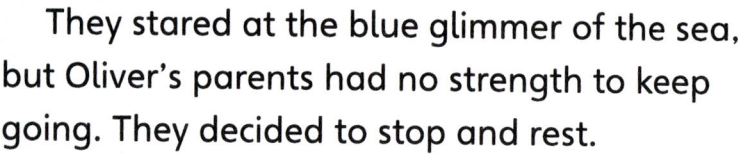

Oliver numbered the trees with his knife. He knew this would help him return to his parents, although what he wanted most right now was time away from them.

The beach yielded nothing except for some kelp and the discarded shell of a sea urchin, but it was wonderful to be beneath the open sky again. He followed the natural curve of the shore to where he had seen the boat vanish with the Garcias on it, and he hit a dead end. The tide was rough here where it crashed upon the coral reefs, but as Oliver turned, the sunlight glanced off something further inland. Suddenly Oliver saw something that made his heart leap.

The Garcias' palm roof had collapsed every one of the fifteen nights they had spent on the island, interrupting any weak dreams they might have managed. There was no rope left to rebuild it with either. Gabriela sighed – the other contestants were in larger groups, with more hands to find food and build shelter. What she forgot, though, was that more hands also meant more mouths to feed.

"Breakfast?" asked her father. The fire was still burning. Mangrove wood produced so much more heat than an ordinary campfire! Her father was trying hard to sound cheerful, but Gabriela was certain the pain in his ankle had kept him awake last night – it looked terrible.

"No, thanks, I'll pass!" she said, scratching at the sand fly bites on her arms. She couldn't bear the thought of any more coconut. "I'll explore further today, Dad, and maybe the tide will bring in something we can use."

Stuck in a town where nothing ever happened, Gabriela couldn't count the number of times she'd dreamed of being on the move, but as she waded away, she heard her father groan in pain. Gabriela wished they were back home. How long could they stay put without food?

The air stank of saltwater and rotting wood. The tree limbs were covered with barnacles, as sharp as knives, and the black mud weighed down Gabriela's feet. It was slow going, and somewhere in these murky depths, she knew there was a saltwater crocodile, or perhaps a sea snake. Suddenly something wrapped itself around her ankles!

It was just a plastic bag. The tide had brought in bottles and cartons, scraps and shreds. Did people give any thought to where their rubbish ended up, Gabriela wondered. Still, one person's waste could be another person's windfall.

Gabriela's eyes fell upon a dented kitchen pan, snagged in the tree roots. She perched on the roots and eased her hand toward it, and then suddenly the sound of squelchy footsteps made her freeze. It was a soft, sly sound . . . there, again! Gabriela's hairs were on end now. She was being watched. She craned her neck and through the thick labyrinth of roots, she could see a – what could it be? *A chain link fence* . . . but she was interrupted by the squelch again!

"Come out if you dare!" she shouted, sounding braver than she felt. And from a small opening in the fence, Oliver emerged.

The Lius had escaped the windswept tundra and were trudging downhill determinedly. They were out of water and conversation when Shen cried out, "Look!"

What had caught Shen's eye was a flash of orange in the distance. He kept his eyes on it for more than ten minutes, and it didn't move.

But the others only had eyes for the heart-lifting sight of mist hanging like a veil over a tree-covered valley.

"Cloud forest!" gasped Mei. Tall ferns fanned out, tangled vines wound their way around moss-clad tree trunks, drops of water nestled in the axils of leaves and trembled on leaf tips. *Everything* was wet.

But after their thirst was quenched came a burning hunger and a bone-aching cold. Mr Liu rushed into a cave, only to be driven out by a colony of bats. Mrs Liu picked a mushroom, but Shen made her throw it away. Wild mushrooms in the cloud forest were probably deadlier than snakes.

Down in the cloud forest, it rained every evening, and even though they had kept their matches dry, the wood was soaked. For three days they lived on orchids and other forest flowers, but the fern fronds they'd picked needed to be boiled first.

After three freezing nights, Shen knew what he had to do. He must find dry kindling for the fire, and food. But first he would retrace his steps to the flash of orange that he had seen the day they had first stumbled upon the cloud forest.

It took some walking, but he found it eventually. It was no bird or forest creature, and that was to be expected; after all, it hadn't moved. But what he hadn't expected was to find an orange harness, strung upon a steel zip wire that disappeared into the forest canopy.

Was this for him? Shen wriggled into the harness and fastened it to the cable. He looked up at the flying cameras hovering overhead and bit his lip; there was only one way to find out.

"So today, all our competitors stepped out of their comfort zones," trilled Berry Blue, in a yellow sarong with butterflies on it. "But is that wise? I guess we'll just have to wait and see!"

CHAPTER FOUR

"It seems that a few of our players have decided to put their heads together and work this out in a civilised way, even if they *are* in the jungle!" Berry Blue's hand flew to her mouth. "But oops, we can't talk about that; it's top secret, after all!"

It was probably a foolish thought, coming this late, but as Shen hurtled down the zip line at more than thirty miles per hour, he wondered how this was going to end. He tried to touch the cable with his hand, but the friction scorched his skin. When would he slow down enough to stop? Would he have to jump?

Meanwhile, Gabriela was jumping – to conclusions. "You're a cheat," she told Oliver, "trying to steal things from our side of the fence!"

Oliver flushed. "I'm only looking for water and a container of some sort . . ." He levelled his gaze at the battered pan in Gabriela's hand, as her fingers tightened around it, and said, ". . . and matches."

Gabriela shook her head in disbelief. "Can't you rich types figure out anything on your own?"

That was when Oliver strode out of the underbrush and grabbed Gabriela by her wrist. "If we were meant to figure out everything on our own, do you think the programme organisers would have cut a neat little rectangle in this fence? It's just large enough for one person to slip through!" he shouted angrily.

Drawing closer to the opening, Gabriela frowned. It did look like it had been cut precisely, not gnawed by animals or worn out by time, but she hung back. "Why would I help you to win?" she asked.

Oliver told her about how Mrs Walpole had spilled her shampoo in a freshwater pool that took them days to find, and how Mr Walpole had scared off a wild hog snuffling for water. "If he'd stayed quiet, the hog would have led us to a dried river bed or a stream, I'm sure!"

Gabriela giggled. "Two parents, twice the trouble?" Oliver's mouth twitched, but before he could chuckle, there was a loud buzzing sound . . . bees? And a high-pitched shriek that sounded nothing like any jungle animal. "Eeeeeeyaaaaaaiiiiii!"

Gabriela ducked, and a pair of flying shoes and dangling legs scuffed the top of Oliver's head.

"Aaaiiii!" A boy shot past them as if on wings and landed with a thud against a tree trunk.

"You made quite an entrance!" exclaimed Gabriela after she and Oliver had followed the zip wire to where it came to a stop.

"I took the scenic route!" Shen grinned, relieved to discover that the zip wire had been fitted with a braking system. He wriggled out of his harness. His legs felt like jelly.

Oliver's face lit up. "By any chance, did you see a river on the way down?"

They each introduced themselves, and Oliver expanded on his parents' mistakes, whilst Gabriela and Shen talked about their families' needs for basic supplies.

After they had all explained their positions, Shen gave Oliver a flask of water from his backpack and some solid advice. "Walk north and you'll hit the river. Use the sun to guide you!" Gabriela and Shen then pooled a few matchsticks for Oliver. Gabriela gave Shen plenty of coconut husks to build a fire with, and in return, Shen gave Gabriela a mosquito net to keep off the sand flies.

"This is all the fruit I'm left with," said Oliver, sharing it with his two newfound friends. At that, Gabriela's face softened. "Take this old pan, it's no use to me anyway! And keep your fruit; we can always eat more coconuts!"

"Looks like they can't do it alone . . ." sang Berry Blue, in a flamingo-pink kaftan now, and here her mouth twisted as her face filled the screen. "Maybe someone needs to tell these people that competitors can't be friends. There's only one prize, after all!"

CHAPTER FIVE

In the cloud forest, the ferns parted to reveal Shen, almost keeling over from the weight of his backpack. It had been a hard climb back to his family – too bad a zip wire couldn't travel upwards.

Mr Liu had a hollow cough now, and Mei had padded her mother's clothes with tufts of cotton from the pods of a silk-cotton tree. The Lius were still cold, and when the coconut husks Shen brought back caught fire with the first strike of a match, they huddled around it silently.

"We'll cross the river into the lowlands tomorrow," Shen told Mei quietly. Mei raised her eyebrows; mountain rivers were notoriously ferocious and fast-flowing.

Then Shen showed her the makeshift rope he had twisted out of stripped bark. "But Mum can't swim!" hissed Mei. Shen then produced the orange harness – they would hitch their parents to the rope and cross the river at its broadest, shallowest point.

"How I got this harness is a long story for when we're out of here!" he said when Mei pressed him for an explanation.

Oliver limped back to his parents with a thermos of water that they fell upon gratefully. "What took you so long?" said Mrs Walpole as soon as she'd caught her breath.

On Shen's advice, the Walpoles moved north slowly, boiling water in the saucepan Gabriela had found, with borrowed matches. Eventually, they found a stream, and that stream led to a larger one, and then down all the way to a river, and to food and water.

"We're safe!" shouted Mrs Walpole, frolicking in the water. "We've done it; I always knew we could!"

Cut off by high tides, Gabriela took the longest to return to camp. Her heart beat faster as she glimpsed her father, crouched at the bank of the swamp. She would tie the spare mosquito net Shen had given her around her father's ankle, and then they could head for the river Shen had told them about.

But when her father turned, he was smiling. "The ankle's much better," he said, "and I've never been happier to see a mosquito net." He showed her why.

Mr Garcia strung their net across the low tide line, as the salty tidal waters washed in, then out, leaving behind a generous catch of fish. "No more coconuts for dinner," he said gleefully, and Gabriela threw her arms around her father as she realised parents could be pretty surprising sometimes.

"Well, here we are on day twenty-one, and our winners have been revealed! It's really no surprise that so many of our viewers voted for the Garcias," said Berry Blue, blowing her nose into a lacy white handkerchief. "There were so many reasons why they deserved to win today: there were only two of them to begin with, and then Mr Garcia was injured and they had to stay put, yet they managed to stay alive. But do you know what I found most winning, and not just me, but all our viewers too?" And here Berry Blue's chin trembled dramatically. "That the Garcias decided to share their prize with the Walpoles and the Lius!"

The flying cameras panned across the beach to where three families were sitting around a fire, cracking open coconuts, barbecuing fish, even laughing.

"In the wild, plants compete for sunlight, and animals compete for food and water," Berry Blue was saying now. "Who would have thought that three children could rewrite the very rules of survival? But they did, and they taught the grown-ups a thing or two about working together, pooling resources, and sharing knowledge."

A fat tear rolled down Berry Blue's perfect cheek. "That's the moral, my friends, for those of us who stayed home on our comfy sofas, watching and voting. It isn't just human beings who survived on this remote island, but humanity too!"